Dedicated to the memory of John Robertson — research

MILLPORT PIER ALBUM

An illustrated popular history or
Some Aspects of Piers and Shipping on Great Cumbrae

by ALASTAIR CHISHOLM

* * *

Front Cover: *A day to remember: Caledonian MacBrayne's ferry "Saturn" re-opens Millport Pier, Saturday 4th April, 1992.* *(Walter Kerr)*

Inside Front Cover: *Waverley arrives at Millport Pier, 2nd August, 1983.* *(Ian A. Duncan)*

Inside Back Cover: Top: : *Looking up the Pier, 25th May, 1964, showing old and new sheds, old and new turnstiles and new pier offices. Piermaster Miller on left.* *(Ian A. Duncan)*

Inside Back Cover: Bottom: *Summer evening about 1959 showing Talisman, Ashton, Saxon, Triumph III and Speedwell.* *(Ian Brown)*
Back Cover: *Visiting fishing boats, 20th August, 1964 with Saxon and Leven or Ashton and McLachlan's green Merlin.* *(Ian A. Duncan)*

"O God of our Salvation, Who art the hope of all the ends of the earth, and of them that remain in the broad sea; we commend to Thy fatherly protection all those who go down to the sea in ships and occupy their business in great waters . . ."

from the Cumbrae Collect (1894)

Published by St. Maura Press :: Printed by Largs Printing Co.
First Published May, 1992

G. & S.W. Glen Rosa passing Outer Eilean showing the rocky hazards of Millport Bay, about 1920.
courtesy McLean Museum

Contents

Queen Mary 11 defies the reputed shallowness of Millport by arriving at low tide, late 1960s. courtesy Walter Kerr.

Preface

MILLPORT PIER! Why a book on Millport Pier? Well, it's a pretty unusual one, with an interesting story. Like the town itself, Millport Pier has just "growed". Like the town too, there has been no attempt to patch over the joins between the work of one generation and another. They are there for all to see. Both town and pier were virtually complete by 1914, and functioned very well till Regionalisation hit the island in 1975. Now thanks to the awareness of the neglect of Cumbrae in the period 1975-85 both are being restored in collaboration with a caring local authority.

For over 150 years almost everyone bound for Cumbrae landed at Millport Pier. It became the social and business hub of the community. It was also used by fishing boats, puffers, cargo steamers and local boathirers. Every aspect of the local community touched on the pier. Newly married couples were given a fine send-off from the Pier by cheering friends and steamer's whistle. The coffin of that great benefactor of Cumbrae, the 6th Earl of Glasgow was landed here on its way to burial at the Cathedral. Local men left from Millport Pier to fight for King and country in two World Wars. Here too on a Saturday evening in September when padella lights twinkled on the promenade, a busy paddle steamer would arrive in the gloaming, carrying crowds from all over the Firth to enjoy the evening of the Millport Illuminations.

Maid of Argyll heads south, late 1960s
courtesy Walter Kerr.

It may seem strange that a book about Millport Pier should be used to raise funds for the Appeal of the Cathedral of The Isles, yet both are special aspects of Millport's heritage. Both have survived despite the odds, and, thanks to Millport people have recently been restored. It seems thus quite fitting to use this little Album for the Appeal. Why not land at Millport Pier and visit Britain's smallest Cathedral?

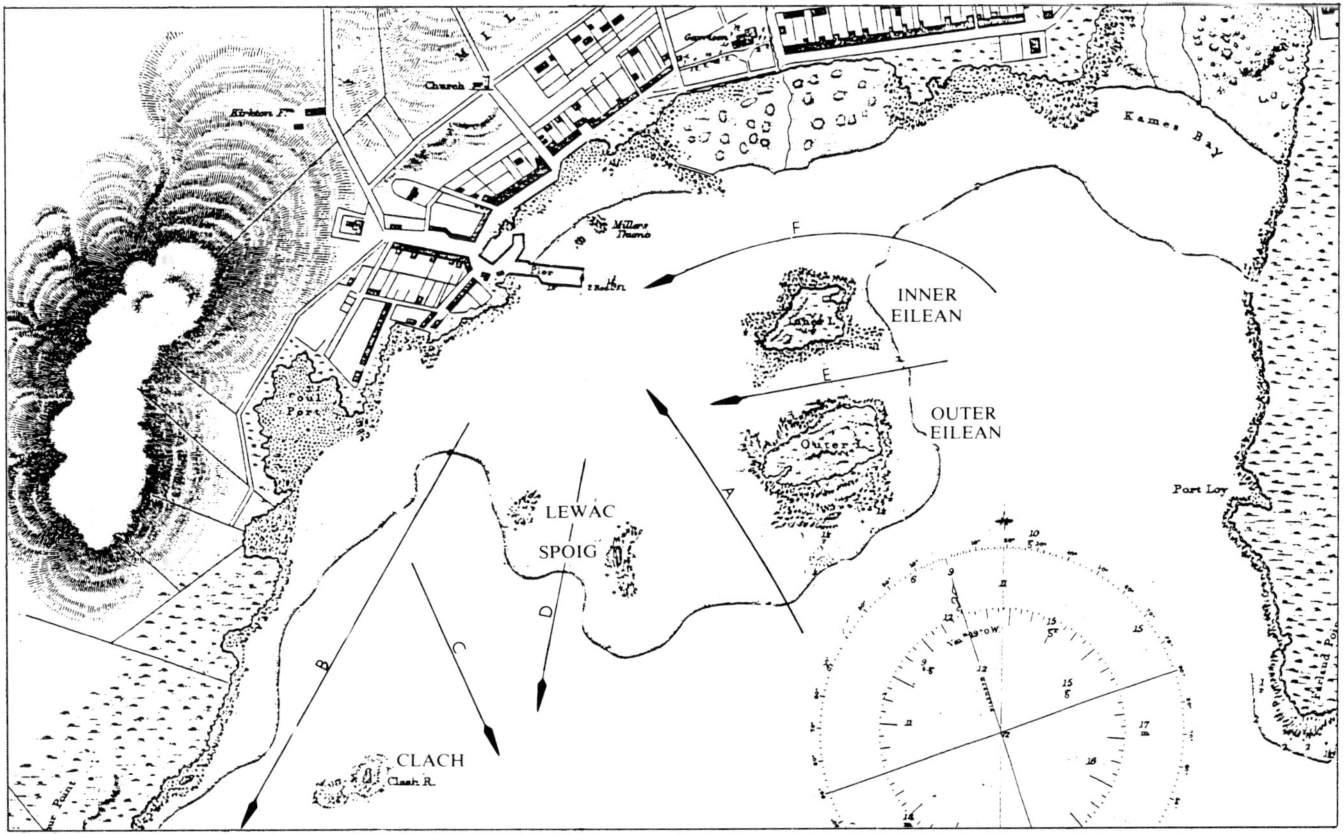
INNER
EILEAN
OUTER
EILEAN
LEWAC
SPOIG
CLACH
Clach R.
Kames Bay
Port Loy
Pier
A
B
C
D
E
F

The Physical Location

MILLPORT BAY is well-known to holidaymakers as a glorious place on a calm summer day. There, the promenaders and the children on the beach can relax and be at their ease while watching the boats sail to and fro. However to the skipper of an approaching steamer, the Bay must offer a different prospect. There are five substantial rocky islands all presenting hazards for the unwary and none of the intervening channels are very deep. Indeed ships which call regularly at Millport Pier should not have a draught greater than seven feet. This of course precludes all the larger Caledonian MacBrayne Clyde ferries, though not their cruise vessel *Keppel*. *Waverley* too is a shallow-draughted ship and has no problems in Millport Bay at low tide.

Marchioness of Graham leaving westwards with Atalanta arriving from the south, 1936.
courtesy Struan Robertson.

There are several possible approaches to the Pier through the various narrow channels and the accompanying map shows them in detail:

(A) is suitable at all tides but at low water the rocky seabed which lies between the Outer Eilean and the Spoig is only seven feet from the surface.

(B) and (C) are suitable at all tides.

(D) and (E) are only suitable for small vessels above mid-tide.

(F) is only suitable at high tide and when cleared of mooring buoys.

Caledonia sails between Inner Eileań and the shore at high tide in winter, 1950s courtesy Walter Kerr.

Early representation of village and harbour, about 1800. from a painting.

Early Days

THE traditional site for the earliest community on Great Cumbrae was at Kirkton (near the Old Cemetery on the present Golf Course Road), and for many years transport to and from the mainland was by road from Kirkton to Balloch Bay and by ferry to Largs or Fairlie. The village of Millport itself did not come into existence till the 18th century. It was only when the Revenue Cutter was based at moorings in what we now call Millport Bay that a community became established there. The Cutter based at Cumbrae was successful at apprehending smugglers, and each new cutter was larger than the previous one. The final one, the largest of all, was a substantial ship of 250 tons called *Royal George*. She had a crew of 60 who needed accommodation on shore near their ship's moorings. Thus the village of Millport was born, and grew.

According to local oral tradition, the earliest harbour was built at the suggestion of Captain Andrew Crawford of the Cutter. It was a by-product of the quarrying activities carried out on an island in Millport Bay, for Portpatrick Harbour. In those days, the ground on which the Royal George Hotel now sits was a rocky off-shore island called Craiglee. At high tide water flowed between Craiglee and the main island. This rock was exploited so thoroughly that eventually it was possible to build an inn on top of it. The spare rock from the quarried island was dumped between Craiglee and the shore to form a permanent link with the main island irrespective of tide. And so the beginnings of Millport Harbour were formed. Certainly by 1772 in John Blane's map it was noted that Millport had a "good working free stone quay."

In the final two decades of the 18th century it was recorded that the population of the island nearly doubled. In 1793 there were 509 people, and one must assume that the village of Millport increased in proportion. Certainly the streets of what we now think of as the old town — Clyde Street, Cardiff Street, Crichton Street, Miller Street — must date from this time. This increasing population made great use of their quay. We know this, because, when, in a storm in 1797, part of it collapsed, it was a local disaster. But there were enough able-bodied men to re-build it both speedily and in an improved form. The Harbour as it appeared after 1797 was much larger than it is today, and much more curved in shape. It included most of the square outside what is now the Royal George Hotel. It was used by local fishermen and sailing smacks, and was an excellent shelter in stormy weather. But the Harbour has always had one great disadvantage — it dries out at low tide.

This was not a matter of great moment until the advent of a regular steamship service in the years following

Pier and harbour, about 1860.

the first appearance of *Comet* in 1812. The expansion of these services was quite remarkable. In the 1820s alone 32 new steamers were built for service on the Firth. A new way of life was coming to the coastal towns. Tourism became an ever more dominant part of the local economics, and the need to make improvements became vital.

On Cumbrae the main arrival point moved from Douncraig in Balloch Bay to Millport Bay. No longer were passengers and goods brought over the hilly Ferry Road. Instead, they sailed directly into Millport Bay, and when the steamers moored inside the Eileans, passengers were landed by small boat at the Strathwherry Pier or at the steps at Knox's Port to the west of the Harbour.

This type of landing must have been uncomfortable, time-consuming, and sometimes dangerous, and the need for a non-tidal landing-place became an increasing necessity. In 1833, the Millport Pier and Harbour Company was formed to erect a Pier which would be accessible to steamers at any stage of the tide. The chairman was Captain James Miller of Millburn, and the Pier built as an arm projecting from the existing Harbour. The landowner, the Marquis of Bute, gave the land free, and also contributed £100 to the scheme. The total cost was £838. The writer of the New Statistical Account in May, 1840, described the recent improvement in communication with the mainland since the diversion of traffic from the Ferry Road to the "fine new pier."

The 1830s, '40s and '50s saw a rapid growth in the village. By 1860 the outline of the front street as we now know it, was in existence. The New Town (towards Kames Bay) had been started, the Crosshouse was begun, the present Parish Church had been built, and the College and Collegiate Church (later the Cathedral) had also been built. The Dowager Countess of Glasgow and one of her sons, George Frederick Boyle, spent much of the year residing in Garrison House, and must have contributed a great deal to the local economy. George Frederick was the founder of the College and Collegiate Church, and, as brother of the Earl of Glasgow, who owned the larger part of the island, he took a great interest in local affairs. His generosity to the already prosperous town ensured his popularity at election, and he became the first Provost when the town was given Burgh status in 1864.

Contemporary with the growth of the town was the increasing size of the steamers serving it. Ships of the 1830s had been about 100 feet long, but twenty years later ships sailing to Millport were almost twice as long. As a result, the approach to the Pier was proving difficult for these larger steamers, so, in 1859, the Pier and Harbour Company planned an enlargement of the 1833 stone Pier, with offices at the head of the Pier close to the town. This work was completed in 1861, and is the basis of the stonework of our present Pier.

One result of the larger Pier was that it provided more shelter from the prevailing winds, and the small boats began to use it instead of the tidal Harbour. There was also a decline in the fishing fleet at this time, so the Harbour was larger than necessary. It was, therefore, decided to infill 31 feet of it in 1872, and this helped to ease the congestion between the Harbour and the Royal George Inn when crowds streamed off the steamers in summertime. The cost of this was £110, and the changes were appreciated thus in the *North British Daily Mail* of 22 June, 1872: "The improvement upon the old harbour does away completely with the stench which formerly existed there, and the addition to the old quay for the loading and unloading of small vessels will do away with the crush that formerly was about the head of the pier." Mention of the "addition to the old quay" would seem to imply that the Mid-Pier, i.e. the outer wall of the Harbour, had been extended. Certainly the shape of the Mid-Pier wall altered at this time. Incidentally, it is not certain whether the "stench" was caused by rotting seaweed, or worse. Millport's sewerage system was very much in its infancy at that time!

The Millport Pier and Harbour Company prospered during the next thirty years. As the number of

Pier from the west, 1878, with the Campbell's Vesta. courtesy McLean Museum.

visitors increased, and the size of the steamers grew, dividends paid to shareholders were high. In 1865, the first railhead steamer connection was made with Wemyss Bay, and in 1882 a summer-only service began from Fairlie Pier. The following year saw the ending of the daily connection direct from the Broomielaw, but at the beginning of the nineties the services from Wemyss Bay and Fairlie were taken over by the railway companies, and soon, new sophisticated ships were competing on the two routes. The Caledonian Steam Packet Company maintained a smaller winter service from Wemyss Bay, but the Glasgow and South Western Railway steamers did not sail from Fairlie in the off-season.

During these years four small changes were made to the structure of the Pier and Harbour. In the early 1880s the Harbour was filled in further "for the safety of the public in the winter months." In the spring of 1889, in common with other Clyde piers, a small white signal box was built to regulate the arrival of competing steamers. The third change, agreed to by the Town Council on April 12, 1898, was the erection of new waiting rooms etc. at the Pierhead. They were built of red sandstone and had a distinctive curved frontage and turret. The final change took place in the early 1900s when there was a further reduction in the size of the harbour, but not this time by means of a direct infill. Instead, stone pillars were sunk at the new limit of the harbour, and a decking built over them. This unusual feature can be seen in many photographs.

During the nineties the Burgh Commissioners (Town Council) became interested in acquiring two local enterprises: the Pier and Harbour Company and the Cumbrae Gaslight Company. Both were seen as profitable enterprises which were vital assets to the town. Despite initial setbacks the Gas Company was bought in 1896, but the Pier Company proved difficult. By April, 1897, the Council's offer of £7500 had been accepted by the Company, but a deputation of Ratepayers voiced their objection to the purchase, and following a plebiscite the proposal was abandoned. Perhaps it was just as well, because in the negotiations it was discovered that the Company's Title Deeds were not in order!

Town and harbour, late 1860s. courtesy of Annan & Co.

Smoky G. & S.W. Marquis of Bute arrives in 1890s showing Pier's first signal cabin. courtesy E. McLaughlan

Disputes and Growth

By 1900, therefore, it was becoming clear that the Pier required further extension. Some of the larger Clyde steamers like the *Jupiter* and even the 1899 *Waverley* were beginning to pay occasional calls on charter, and it must have been very difficult to berth such large ships at the existing Pier, particularly at low tide. Following an internal financial re-organisation the Pier and Harbour Company made preliminary plans for a pier extension. To help pay for the work, it was decided to increase the dues paid by steamers. Annual costs for the Caledonian Steam Packet Company steamers were to rise from £195 to £250, and for the Glasgow and South Western Company steamers from £180 to £200. Negotiations were protracted. The steamer companies claimed that the traffic would not bear this additional cost, but the Pier Company refused to accept this. They pointed out that more than ten years previously, Captain Campbell, owner of the Wemyss Bay steamers, had paid £230 per annum for a smaller number of calls. Why should they, the CSP, now pay less? The G.&S.W. Company, on the other hand, claimed that they now paid twice what their predecessors had paid for their Fairlie steamers, so why should they pay still more? Uncharacteristically, the two Companies joined forces against the Pier Company and refused to pay the increased dues. They announced that they would both withdraw from the Old Pier before 1st June, 1901, but would continue to serve Keppel Pier.

This eventuality had been foreseen by the Millport Pier and Harbour Company, and, to avoid the diversion of all the island's traffic to Keppel, they had negotiated a lease of that pier from its owners for 3 years from April, 1901. At least they thought they had, until the Keppel Pier Company received the same notice of withdrawal of services as had the Old Pier. At this point the Keppel Pier Company repudiated any lease agreement, and it was announced that the steamers would continue to call at Keppel. Enraged at what they must have felt as betrayal, the Millport Pier and Harbour Company sued the Keppel directors. The feud was eventually settled out of court.

Clearly, all this acrimony would not encourage vistors to the island. Certainly the early part of the 1901 season had been pretty quiet. The International Exhibition in Glasgow was blamed for attracting potential customers away from the coastal towns. As a result, the Town Council sent a deputation to mediate between the warring parties, and eventually the Pier Company backed down and the old dues were restored.

The whole incident must have greatly perturbed local business people, and it was obviously unsatisfactory that such an important service as the Piers should be in

Building of the Extension, spring 1906. courtesy Museum of the Cumbraes

the hands of two independent companies. It was time that they were controlled by the Town Council who would act for the benefit of the whole town.

On the island there was certainly much dissatisfaction with the dealings of the Millport Pier and Harbour Company. Many felt that the Company's shareholders were benefitting from a "gold mine", and that as little as possible was being spent on the maintenance and improvement of the Pier. After the debacle of 1901 a committee was appointed to re-investigate the feasibility of purchasing the Pier. As before, the principal problem was the lack of complete title deeds. After consultation with the Marquis of Bute and lawyers, it was arranged that he would buy Millport Pier and Harbour from the private Company for £5000 and sell it in turn, now with the proper Title, for the same fee, to Millport Town Council. The Council promoted a Bill in Parliament which allowed them to make this purchase, and to make provision for an extension, with powers to raise money for the transactions. Using a similar device, they were also able to buy Keppel Pier. The Act was entitled "Millport Piers and Burgh Extension Confirmation Act, 1905".

At this time Millport Pier was not in very good condition. Evidently there was fairly urgent repair needed to the seaward end with an estimated cost of about £500. Instead of doing this, the Council decided to proceed immediately with the Extension and Renovation for which powers to borrow money had just been given by the Act. It was a complex business, with the outer half of the Pier being widened westward by concrete, and an open timber structure added to lengthen the whole by more than one hundred feet. The reasons for building the extension of wood rather than stone are not certain, but I suspect that the nature of the seabed would be one. Certainly eighty years later, when there was a plan to replace the 1906 timber extension by a solid structure, sheet-piled with a rock infill, the softness of the sea bottom was given as the reason for abandoning the plan. Apparently rock rubble poured between the sheet piles would have continued to sink for an uncertain time.

Perhaps this had been deduced in 1905 and the lighter timber structure was the result. A lattice timber structure does have considerable advantages. With its degree of "give", it is kinder on ships berthing in rough weather. It also presents a much less solid resistance to the power of waves than does a solid structure. Yet it greatly reduces water turbulence on the lee side without forcing the waves over the decking. Some interesting photographs of Millport Pier show heavy seas breaking over the stone section, while passing below the wooden decking and through the piles of the timber extension. On the rare occasions when high tides and southerly gales coincided and the whole Pier was submerged, the timber decking would float off, thus minimising the damage to the rest of the timber structure. It was for this reason that the wooden decking was never bolted in place, but merely wedged. After such bad weather the Council workmen would simply collect the planks from the beach, and return them to their allotted places.

The extension was completed by the addition of a neat new signal cabin with a jaunty red peaked roof. Near the Pier Offices three-lane pedestrian turnstiles were built, and a couple of years later Provost Cockburn presented a turret clock which fitted neatly and conspicuously on top of them.

For much of the construction period, 1905-1906, Millport Pier was closed to steamers, but at Easter it was opened from 13th to 17th April in its incomplete state. Anxiety was expressed by the Council about public liability, but despite efforts to procure insurance cover, no firm would oblige. Fortunately Piermaster Caldwell organised the movements of passengers efficiently and no accidents occured.

Completion was expected by 18th May, by which time there was local disquiet concerning the cost, which now amounted to £9000. One suggestion to re-coup some of the cost was to apply to Lord Bute for permission to charge a penny for each passenger who used the Pier. It was also felt that steamer companies should pay more for calls. It was this attempt to raise more money from the railway steamers that led to all the 1906 trouble.

As before, the railway companies refused to pay the increased rates viz. C.S.P. £400 and Glasgow and South Western Company £362. Millport folk felt that the railways were behaving impudently. It had been worked out that their cost per call was 1/6d, which was less than was paid by a coal boat. Locals just could not comprehend the railways' claim that these increases could not be afforded. When the two companies advertised in the national press on 23rd June that, with effect from Monday 2nd July, their steamers would call at neither Millport nor Keppel Piers, the fat was in the fire.

Local gossip was rife. Ex-Baillie Hunter, who had been Chairman of the old Pier Company during the previous dispute, claimed that the railways were bluffing once more, as he claimed they had been in 1901. It was said that the railways had requested the pier extension, and to refuse the new rates was thus doubly outrageous. As they were paying £740 and £720 respectively in Rothesay, it was felt that the Millport rates were quite reasonable. And so it went on.

As June moved to a close the tension grew. On Wednesday 27th June interest in the dispute spread beyond Scotland. In Parliament, questions on the subject were answered by the President of the Board of Trade, Mr Lloyd George. By this time a Millport Committee, led by Provost Rowatt, was in London talking with Board of Trade officials. Representatives of the two railway companies were there too. Also by this time, the Town Council's offer that the dispute be taken to arbitration, had been flatly refused by the railways.

A ratepayers' meeting was called in Millport for the Friday afternoon. Chairman Baillie Reid read letters from the Provost and Town Clerk about their negotiations in London. A counter-proposal had come from the railway companies that existing rates be paid until October, 1907, and that, while steamers continued to run, further discussions could take place. The Town Clerk felt that this was merely putting off the evil hour. He responded by suggesting that the companies increase their fares by one penny per passenger, and thus cover the higher pier dues. The companies would not countenance this, saying that the service did not pay as it was, and offered instead to sell their steamers to the Council.

At this point it was felt important to involve the ratepayers in the decision-making. The afternoon meeting was drawn to a close, but was to re-convene in the evening, when a telegram from the Provost was read. In it he expressed confidence in the success of the negotiations, and the meeting endorsed the Committee's handling of the affairs, and gave its members the power to bring the matter to a satisfactory conclusion.

The town was very busy on Saturday, June 30th. The question on everyone's lips was: "Would the boats go off?" Most thought not, but when the last steamer called, all railway gangways were uplifted from the Pier. As *Vulcan* and then the *Marchioness of Bute* left for the mainland, the Pier was busy with onlookers, mostly sober and elderly folk. When the *Marchioness of Breadalbane* and finally *Vulcan* left to spend the weekend at Kilchattan Bay, "Auld Lang Syne" could be heard from the onlookers on the pier, and the steamers replied with loud blasts on their whistles.

Sunday, 1st July, brought with it a day of hurried preparation. Normally Millport observed the Sabbath calm, then usual all over Scotland, when no steamers sailed anyway. This Sunday was very different. Council officials were very busy making alternative transport arrangements for the following day. Even the Town Bellman broke the custom by making the announcement that on Monday coaches would leave for Balloch Bay and a motor launch connection to Largs at 6 a.m. At the same time a puffer would leave Millport Pier for Fairlie.

On Monday, 2nd July, Millport rose early. The sea was like glass, though there was a mist which occasionally swelled to rain. The first travellers left by private boat at 4a.m., and by 5.30a.m. the seafront was busy and the Pier crowded. Baillie Reid acted as admiral and all went well. Millport rose to the occasion with what would later be called the "Dunkirk spirit". The water remained perfect, and the service was continued until Tuesday evening, although the puffers were withdrawn after one day when the Board of Trade Inspectors became alarmed at the numbers they were carrying.

It was estimated that over 150 people had travelled to Largs by motor boat from Balloch Bay. Mail was landed by C.S.P. steamers, using lifeboats on Monday. Newspapers were carried from Largs by Mr D. M. Dutch, who also carried passengers in his motor boats. Mr

Knox, the Fairlie boat-hirer, was also busy carrying passengers and several cargoes of potatoes.

C.S.P. steamers continued to call at Largs, but the excursion paddler, *Duchess of Hamilton*, had to make a special arrangement. Largs passengers wishing to join her excursion were usually scheduled to board the C.S.P. Millport steamer at Largs and disembark at Keppel where the *Duchess* would collect them. This arrangement saved the C.S.P. the £2.10s due charged by the owners of Largs Pier, the G.&S.W.R. In chaotic circumstances that week the exchange of passengers once took place in mid-channel! It is interesting to note that G.&S.W. charged £2.10s for a call at Largs, but thought that 1/6d was enough to pay for a call at Millport.

On Tuesday a telegram from Provost Rowatt announced a settlement, and that steamers should be expected the next day. Prudently Baillie Reid ensured that the small boats would be available on the Wednesday morning, just in case, so, when the steamers failed to appear, due to a misunderstanding, the little ships once more stepped in. However the fun was wearing a bit thin by Wednesday evening, and the locals were glad when normality returned on Thursday morning. The settlement which had been achieved was a return to the status quo for both the railway companies and the Council until 15th May, 1907. But negotations for the rates beyond that date began immediately.

Crowds landing showing stone supports for pavement over the harbour, 1908-22. courtesy Walter Kerr

Duchess of Fife and Leven or Ashton on a rough day, c. 1950. courtesy Walter Kerr

Twentieth Century

Since the building of the timber Extension, in 1906, the Pier has remained largely unchanged. Some time after the First World War a goods shed was added beside the signal cabin. This was used as a short-term storage area for the cargo from the ships of Clyde Cargo Steamers Ltd.

The original sea wall along Stuart Street, which had been built in the late 1860s, had become a matter of recurring concern during the 1920s. It had been built piecemeal, and was not an adequate defence in times of storm. The gale of November 1912 had shown how poor it was as a storm defence. On this occasion Stuart Street was deep in water, shops were flooded, and sea water flowed through the tenement closes. A new wall was the only satisfactory solution and this was done in 1929. At the same time, Stuart Street was broadened considerably, and the combined work provided a much better protection against the worst gales. Some changes occurred to the Harbour at the same time. The west end of the Harbour, which had been open, with stone columns supporting the pavement and road surface, allowing the tide to flow below, was given a solid stone finish in the same style as the new sea wall. The weighbridge was moved from the head of the inner pier to a more useful place between the Mid-Pier and the turnstiles, and a new Avery weighbridge was bought.

During World War Two, the Pier staff began to operate a Cartage Department after the Council had bought Stewart's haulage business. This began in 1941 and was a profitable part of the Pier enterprise for many years. In 1945 the Pier's crane was replaced by a Butters' one-ton crane.

The next change came in the 1950s when the wear and tear of the ever larger steamers and the vehicular traffic since 1957, began to tell on the structure, and, in September, 1959, repairs costing £15,000 were agreed to by the Town Council. The Pier buildings and 1898 offices were beginning to show their age, and it was decided to replace most of them in 1962. First to go were the turnstiles. The clock had been removed by New Year 1964, and the new turnstiles placed closer to the offices. Staff moved into the offices in February 1964, and the new goods shed became available at the same time. Although the old goods shed disappeared shortly afterwards, the signal cabin survived all the earlier buildings.

Following an agreement with the coast resorts, passenger pier dues were incorporated into the tickets of the C.S.P., hence the new turnstiles were obsolete shortly after their introduction.

Another improvement made in the 1960s was the construction of steps inside the wooden section. This allowed passengers, for the first time, to have easy access to launches and other small boats, at any state of the tide. Previously, access had been by means of spike ladders. These new steps did not project beyond the coping of the inner berths, so these could still be used by larger vessels when required. These new steps were also used for the overnight removal of seriously ill patients, and were convenient for boat-hirers. An increasing use of them was made by Mr Kaye, owner of Wee Cumbrae.

Throughout the changes in steamer services during the late sixties and early seventies, the Pier continued as before, but the approach of Regionalisation determined the Town Council to spend their remaining funds on important local projects, and in 1973 a major overhaul of the Pier was instigated. Considerable re-piling was undertaken and longitudinal rubber fenders were added to the south-east face. This time the 1906 signal box did not survive. It was disturbed by accident and a new smaller replacement had to be constructed. When Millport Pier was handed over to the new Local Authority in 1975 it was in excellent condition. All that should have been needed was regular maintenance of the timber section, which was standard for a structure of its kind.

Unfortunately, Strathclyde Regional Council adopted a rather negative attitude towards Millport Pier. They spent as little as possible in its maintenance. Soon cross-members and diagonals, which had worked loose, were left and allowed to fall to the seabed. The complex structure of the timber extension was gradually weakened by sheer neglect. In the years after Regionalisation the heavy strain of large vessels calling on the Pier in bad weather had gone. The only large vessel now using it was the paddle steamer *Waverley*, and she called only three days a week for an eight-week summer season. Yet by the end of 1984 Strathclyde's engineers were able to advise their masters that

Harbour showing new sea wall and Little's "Grace", c.1930. courtesy Museum of the Cumbraes.

Waverley had too much weight for the ailing Pier. She was allowed to call only once in 1985 — at the September Weekend. *Keppel's* summer ferry service from Largs ended the same year. She was replaced indirectly by new ships with extra passenger accommodation on the Cumbrae Slip run. Strathclyde's policy under Malcolm Waugh seemed to be to allow Millport Pier to fall apart.

However they reckoned without the determination of local opinion, and soon the future of the Pier was the main topic for discussion at all Community Council meetings. A Pier Committee was formed. Help was sought from all sources. Even the M.E.P., Hugh McMahon, was contacted and pleas were made in Strasbourg. Initially there was no success at all. The fact that Millport Pier was not designated as a "transport pier" seemed to be all-important. Every man's hand in local government was against the Committee, because, like so many things in Cumbrae, it did not fit the neat compartments of the economist's mind. Because of the different budgets involved, it was possible for the University Marine Station to obtain money to replace Keppel Pier, and likewise much money was spent building the National Water Sports Centre north of Balloch Bay. Yet nothing could be found for the Pier which so ostentatiously dominated the centre of Millport and would be used by most people.

During the late 1980s, the Committee tried strategy after strategy. Strathclyde were now keen to rid themselves of the Pier altogether, and in desperation the local Pier Committee contemplated forming a trust to buy the Pier themselves and changing it to a marina. In 1988, however, the S.D.A. became interested, and, in conjunction with Cunninghame District Council, a more publicly acceptable plan was devised, which involved a return to the traditional uses of the Pier by all types of vessels: large excursion vessels, fishing boats, small boats, visiting yachts etc. More facilities for the latter were thought necessary, and in an attempt to retain something of the marina idea, floating pontoons

Social exchange before the boat goes, Duchess of Fife about to leave, 1952. courtesy Ian Brown

Millport Pier in the late 1970s showing Waverley, Keppel, Kestrel and Hilda. N.B. the 1974 signal cabin, now gone.

were to be moored inside the inner berth of the wooden extension. These could be used by yachts for landing and overnight mooring.

Several different plans were proposed for the renovation or replacement of the 1906 extension. One involved a sheet-pile 6-metres broad extension with a dog-leg at the end. Eventually it was deduced that the simplest option was to renovate the existing timber structure.

The notorious storm and high tides of January 5th, 1991 once more lifted the decking of the Pier. This time there was no attempt to replace the planks. The Pier was closed. Even the ever-faithful *Keppel* could not call that summer. Somehow access for Mr Kaye was maintained, and the fishing boats continued to berth overnight. "Walking the plank" must have taken on a new meaning for the crew of the *Nancy Glen* that year.

However, deliverance was at hand. Cunninghame District Council agreed to buy the Pier from the Regional Council, with the proviso that the newly-formed Highland and Islands Enterprises (successor to the S.D.A.) would fund the renovations needed. The empty 1964 Pier Offices were to be transformed into a chandlery and stores for visiting yachtsmen, and a local company, Millport Pier and Harbour Company, would run the Pier for the District Council. And so a name was revived!

In December, 1991, the work on the timber extension was well on. The first larger ship to call at the Pier was the puffer, *Marsa,* in unusual circumstances. She was being towed from Paisley Harbour to the Maritime Museum at Irvine, when bad weather forced her along with her tug (a harbour launch) into Millport. With the help of Stuart McIntyre she was successfully moored at the old cargo berth for a few days before completing her journey to Irvine.

The final work on the timber section was the installation of a hydraulic ramp to give access to the floating pontoons on the inner berth. This was installed in early March, 1992, and the moorings for the pontoons were fixed by an Oban firm at the same time. Work has been done on the stone section too. Both the inner and mid quays have had extensive repairs, and in the case of the mid quay, this has involved the complete re-building of the east end.

The restoration of Millport Pier has therefore been a tremendous achievement. To have done it in a time of recession, when all aspects of government are under pressure, is truly remarkable. Highland Enterprise, Cunninghame District Council, and M.P. Brian Wilson have all played important roles in the process. Most important, however, were members of the Committee, who ploughed onwards through the dark days of the mid-eighties, when many a realist would have given up. All praise to them for their tenacity and vision. The rest of us will now enjoy the results of their endeavours.

Good luck to the Millport Pier and Harbour Company.

The Steamers — a few snippets

THIS is not the place for a detailed history of the steamers sailing to Millport. That can be found elsewhere — in Ian Brown's articles and in Ian McCrorie's booklet "The Millport Route" published by the Clyde River Steamer Club in 1974. Instead I'll present a series of anecdotes, some personal, some not.

From *The History of the County of Bute* by Eaton Reid (1864): "I am informed by Mr John Jamieson, harbourmaster, Millport, that he remembers the appearance of the first steamer at Cumbray — it was the *Comet* — in the summer of 1812, which came from Largs on a Sunday. She lay between the shore and the Allans. About half a dozen people landed from her, and among others, Mr Robert Ewing, farmer, Balloch, then commander of the Cumbray volunteers. After remaining more than half an hour in the bay, she went off round the Portahaur Point towards Rothesay. Some of the inhabitants went out in boats to see her, and many ran up the hills to watch her as she steamed over to Bute. The second steamer which appeared at Millport was the Glasgow (Captain Cook), built in 1813, 64 tons and 14 horse-power. She was the first which plied between Glasgow and Largs and came over to Millport for the benefit of the anchorage. She went up to Glasgow one day and down the next, suiting her times to the tide. She had no mast, but sometimes hoisted a large square sail on the funnel."

From *Largs Advertiser* October 2nd 1875: "At Millport a number of small boats were driven ashore, and the steamer *Lancelot* was compelled to leave the end of the pier and seek refuge in Balloch Bay."

From *Largs & Millport Weekly News*, 28th April 1877: "The Wemyss Bay Steamboat Company are laying down waterpipes from the burn at the head of Cardiff Street to the quay for the supply of their steamers. Millport people are much interested in the new *Sheilah* (sic). The arrangements of this Company last summer gave the utmost satisfaction to the great majority of visitors to the town."

From the *Largs & Millport Weekly News*, 28th April 1877: "The Wemyss Bay Steamboat Company have sold their well-known steamer, *Largs*, to the Waterford Steam Ship Company (Limited). While not exactly a summer favourite, the *Largs* was a very handy boat for the winter traffic and able to make the runs with great regularity when a boat of lighter build would have been unable to run, and winter travellers to and from the coast will miss the old Largs."

From *Largs & Millport Weekly News*, 23rd February 1878: "While the steamer *Argyle* was on her

Pier and harbour, 1876, with Argyle (outside) and Lancelot George Washington Wilson

last run from Wemyss Bay to Millport on Monday evening, and about mid-channel betwixt Fairlie and the Farland Point, her shaft broke with a crash and brought her to a standstill. The night being fine, and there being little sea on, there was no excitement on board. The accident was observed from Fairlie and the ferry-boat went immediately to her assistance, took off the passengers, and landed them safely about the Lion Rock. The *Lancelot* arrived next morning and took the place of the *Argyle.*"

From my memory of Ian Brown's account: "Approaching Millport Pier in southerly winds is often difficult. Each skipper developed his own way of coping. Captain Ferguson on *Marchioness of Breadalbane* in the 1930s had a unique solution. When his steamer was more than halfway across the bay he turned sharply south for a distance and then went astern through the gap between the Outer Eilean and the Spoig. His reasoning was, that wherever he could put the *Breadalbane* stern first, he could more easily sail her out ahead!"

"My first Clyde steamer was *Marchioness of Lorne* in the summer of 1953 when we holidayed at Fairlie. The following spring the family bought a holiday flat in Millport and to my delight we sailed on the *Marchioness* again when we visited for weekends. On Friday evenings we sailed via Wemyss Bay and, on Sunday, back via

Talisman at her adopted home, 1956-59. courtesy Ian Brown.

Fairlie. This seemed to happen several times, but on one Friday the steamer waiting for us at Wemyss Bay was *Caledonia* and to me, as a seven year old steamer nutter, this was very exciting, for I could run round the upper deck, something not possible on the *Marchioness*. We disembarked at Millport and she sailed on as usual to Kilchattan Bay. My weekend of surprises was not over though, for the following morning I was woken by a strange noise coming from the direction of the Pier. A glance showed a steamer that I had never seen before with her bows facing out from the Pier. She had real paddleboxes, the first I'd encountered. Later that day she returned and I discovered that she was diesel electric and was called *Talisman* and it was in this way that I was introduced to what would become one of my favourite ships. My childish memory of these details was confirmed 25 years later. I told the story to Sween MacSween who had been mate on *Talisman* in the 50s. He confirmed that when *Talisman* had been re-engined in 1954 there had been a few teething problems and that *Caledonia* had filled in for a day or two, but very late on that Friday evening *Talisman* had sailed from Gourock direct to Kilchattan Bay in time to take up the run on the Saturday morning."

"The approach to Millport on our own boat, *Talisman*, was always so interesting. After passing the Lion Rock and Keppel Pier, suddenly we had a first glimpse of Millport over the low headland of Farland Point. There was always the chance of "a heave" at Farland because of the meeting of tides there. By then our eyes were fixed on the rapidly unfolding panorama of the Bay, with the neat houses behind the Eileans and the sparkling deep blue water of the Bay in front. As we became aware of the channel between the Outer Eilean and the Spoig the ship swung to starboard and lined up to sail through the gap. Our speed was diminished by the starboard turn, though the engine maintained full speed until we passed the Outer Eilean beacon, after which we made another sharp turn, to port, to line up with the "deep berth". As our bow passed the end of the Pier, full astern was rung and the paddles kicked up

Marchioness of Lorne, canting 1953. Ian Brown

Busy times at the Pier, 1952, showing Waverley and Duchess of Hamilton (outside) with Leven or Ashton. Also goods shed and lorry loading. courtesy Ian A. Duncan.

Ashton high and dry beside Saxon in the harbour, 27th September, 1964 courtesy I. McCrorie.

a froth of white water till we stopped and lines were secure. We had arrived at *Talisman's* adopted home and ours!"

From my memory of Sween MacSween's account: "In midsummer when *Talisman's* hull was becoming weedy, in an attempt to maintain speed, we tried to remove some of the growth on the Millport sand. The best time to arrange this was on alternate Sunday lunch times if the tide was rising. On our approach to Millport we would not use as much astern power as usual. Consequently, she was stopped by the sand, and in the process we had rubbed off most of the weed. By the time an hour had elapsed she was afloat and ready to sail again — faster!"

"Winter Sundays in the 1950s were always interesting because of the weekly appearance of a paddler after a week of *Maids* or worse. On those days either *Caledonia* or *Talisman* sailed from Gourock via Dunoon and Rothesay to Fairlie and Millport arriving there at 1 o'clock. After spending three hours at Cumbrae she left for the return trip. This was the only boat at Millport on a winter Sunday at that time. Strangely though, it became a very social occasion. If the weather was at all decent quite a number of locals would come down to enjoy the scene. Weekenders would be returning to the city, local teenagers would be crossing to Rothesay to continue their secondary schooling. There was much gossip, banter and good humour until sailing time came. The wheels turned, the bow eased out, ropes

Accident. Cowal missing the Pier, July, 1967. courtesy Walter Kerr.

plashed in the water and away she went, in a flutter of waving and greetings."

Leven and *Ashton* were the least pretentious craft owned by the C.S.P. and they were a lot of fun to sail on. They were the only "steamers" which regularly sailed between the Inner and Outer Eileans and I have even seen one sail inside the Inner Eilean in summer at high tide, carefully avoiding the moored small craft. Another curiosity about "the ferries" was their occasional appearance in the Harbour at weekends. Each was given a Sunday maintenance day every fortnight and if the tide was suitable, they were brought into the Harbour on Saturday night. On Sunday afternoon small boys enjoyed walking beneath the exposed hulls. When they sailed round Farland Point they usually gave a much "livelier" passage than the larger ships. The best vantage points were the platforms either side of the bridge or the little lowered deck aft. The fare was less than on the regular ships, but even so we still tried to dodge paying by jouking into the toilets when the "conductor" came round to issue tickets. *Leven* and *Ashton* were excellent sea boats, and one was often used in winter as mail and newspaper boat for the island. Today they are the sole operational survivors of the pre-war C.S.P. fleet and continue to sail in English waters.

"One July afternoon in 1967 I witnessed a steamer accident at Millport Pier. In retrospect it shows how little room for error there is in any approach to the Pier. The car ferry *Cowal* was approaching and was lining up to berth along the short south east face, with the bows pointing towards the Miller's Thumb. I was watching as she edged close to the Pier, but at the last moment that her engines should have gone to full astern, they seemed instead to go to full ahead. She shot past the pier and before she could be stopped, her bow had struck the Miller's Thumb. She lost a rudder. Fortunately she was quickly manoeuvred back to the Pier and was able to complete her day's outing, but it was a close thing."

"That year saw the first season of the *Keppel* and we did not like her initially. She was so slow — worse than *Countess of Breadalbane* and not nearly so pretty. She was seen by the C.S.P. as a partial replacement for my favourite *Talisman* so I was prejudiced against her from the start. However she settled down on the run and soon became the regular winter boat too. The saloons downstairs were pretty barren and gloomy, and she was not very warm in December, yet it was in this role she gave her finest service. In her first three winters she did not miss a single scheduled run. Her great manoeuverability gave her an advantage over larger vessels in rough weather at the piers. Of course her reliability would not have meant anything, had she not had a fine crew including men like Donald MacLeod, Calum Morrison, Alistair MacMillan and Angus McInnes. They worked hard to make *Keppel* accepted and they succeeded. It is a sobering thought that *Keppel* has been closely associated with Millport and its Pier for 25 years. Not bad for a Tilbury ferryboat!"

Harbour, 1890s shows Mary Kerr. courtesy Annan & Co.

The Cargo Boats

THE earliest known report of cargo vessels sailing from Cumbrae comes in a series of Government reports, among which is listed the sailing from Cumbrae of eleven vessels between 1707 and 1712. At least three of these vessels would have been decked: *Mary I*, 30 tons; *Robert*, 36 tons; *William*, 36 tons; the others would be smaller open sailing fishing boats. A newspaper of 3rd March, 1712, reported that "One (French) cutter took the *Providence of Cumbrass* from Dublin with leather, 40 tons, Robert Montgomery, and ransomed her at the 'back of the land' (Luce Bay) for £40 and 2 guineas." It is not certain whether these early ships were based at Millport, or if they were moored elsewhere on the island.

Duncan Campbell tells us "One of the earlier ventures of cargo-carrying between the islands in the Firth and Greenock was by a vessel called *The Nimble* in 1811. She was owned by a company of local men — John Finnie of Mid Kirkton, Robert Ewing of Ballochmartin and John Hunter who was the master of The Nimble. *The vessel had an interesting history being a Dutch fishing smack captured in the North Sea on December 12, 1809 by the British armed cutter H.M.S. Albion*. She was in Burntisland for two years after being sold at a Prize Court and then came to Millport. Her cargo capacity was about 30 tons."

About 1870 a local fisherman, Walter Kerr, decided to become involved in cargo-carrying to the island. Presumably he began by using an old fishing boat. Certainly he was a skilled sailor as he was noted in the Western Yacht Club notes of May, 1878, as skippering the yacht, *Polly,* which led throughout, "being splendidily steered by Walter Kerr".

Perhaps, like many Millport boatmen, he spent time working as a yacht crew for the wealthy visitors. By 1880 he was ready to order a new smack for the cargo trade. This order went to Fyfe of Fairlie, and the result was the *Jessie Kerr*, costing £250 complete with sails and gear. Fyfe is reputed to have said to the *Jessie Kerr's* owner, "Walter, when you ordered this boat it would have paid me to have given you £10 and sent you away." So perhaps he had under-estimated the cost of construction! The boat was clearly a splendid acquisition and Kerr went back to Fyfe a few years later for a second sailing smack — the *Mary Kerr* — which was likewise a great success. The two Kerr ships sailed together till the 1900s. Their main cargo was coal, for both domestic and Gas Company use. On occasion too they took bulk cargoes to and from the farms at the north end of the island, though whether they used Balloch Bay Pier, Tattie Pier or Figgatoch Farm jetty, is not clear.

The *Mary Kerr* was sold to an Arran owner in the 1900s, and lasted with various owners until after World War II. The "Jessie Kerr" came to grief on rocks near Horse Island while entering Ardrossan Harbour in 1912. As a replacement, Walter's son, Finlay, bought the 56 foot fifie yawl, *The Sisters,* for £30 from east coast owners, and had her converted to a cargo ketch at Ardmaleish on Bute. Called *Betty Kerr*, she had an auxiliary engine and carried on a similar trade to that of the earlier Kerr boats.

The sailing smacks and the *Betty Kerr* had a cargo capacity of 30 tons, and something larger was needed by the early 1920s. All over the firth, sailing vessels were giving way to the steam lighters, known as puffers, and so it was at Millport. The puffer *Saxon* (originally *Dane*, built in 1903 at J. and J. Hay's yard at Kirkintilloch) had sunk off Greenock on 3rd December, 1925. Finlay Kerr and his son, Walter, bought her as she was, raised her and re-furbished her in time to begin trading in May, 1926. With a carrying capacity of 80 tons and a reliable steam engine, she gave a greatly improved service for the bulk goods to Cumbrae. In Millport she became an institution, part of the apparently unchanging Millport scene. Much of her time was spent in the Harbour, berthed against the Mid-quay, where she lay aground at every low tide. Latterly her principal cargoes were coal from Troon for the island's Gasworks, and coke and tar from these works to Rothesay Dock,

Saxon cants into harbour, about 1960. Author.

Clydebank. Most of her unloading was carried out at the inner berth of the Main Pier using her own donkey engine and winch. Her single bucket was shovel-filled, and lifted by derrick to the quayside in an enveloping cloud of steam. Even in her later years, Walter Kerr would still use the auxiliary sail as a help in a suitable wind. Her most famous later work was in the television series of Para Handy, for which she was renamed *Vital Spark*. However the end came in 1966 when Kerr sold her for scrap and sailed her to Greenock. My last sight of her was in the harbour there in Spring, 1967, looking very pale-funnelled and a rusty contrast to the smart, scarlet and black feature of Millport Harbour that we all knew and loved so well.

Puffers continued to supply the island's coal after the departure of the *Saxon*, but they were not owned by islanders. *Lady Isle*, *Lady Morvern*, *Spartan* and *Anzac* were among the vessels which served us. They were diesel-powered, large-capacitied, faster and had a mechanical grab which eased considerably the labour of unloading them in port. However, when the *Isle of Cumbrae* was placed on the Largs-Cumbrae Slip service, the heavy traffic was diverted to lorries which could easily use the larger ferry and eliminate the labour costs inherent in the puffer trade.

Until the 1870s general cargo was presumably brought to the island by steamer or sailing smack. From at least 1877 the small cargo steamer *Success*, owned by

Largs fishing boat lands party with Bute 4 in background, 1920s.
courtesy Museum of the Cumbraes.

Hill and Company, ran a twice-weekly cargo service from Glasgow to coast towns including Largs and Millport. *Success* was a small ship about the size of a puffer, although differently laid out. She was joined by the somewhat larger steamer *Bute* in 1881. The two seem to have run together for a year till the disposal of *Success*. By the 1900s the same company was in operation now, running the 115 foot *Bute 4* thrice weekly service to the coast from the city. *Bute 4* became well-known on the run and lasted till 1935. Hill and Co. had been amalgamated with other small cargo ship companies to form Clyde Cargo Steamers Ltd. in August 1915 and other ships of the company like *Ardyne* and *Arran* probably sailed to Millport from time to time.

In November, 1949, the *Arran*, a 120 foot cargo steamer with machinery aft, took over the Arran and Millport services from Ardrossan, with railway connections to Glasgow. The service was thrice weekly, but was not profitable. By this time the Company had been renamed Clyde and Campbeltown Shipping Company, and was, from 1949 onwards, a subsidiary of British Rail. On the commission of the new general purpose ferry *Arran*, the cargo steamer was re-named *Kildonan*, and as such she continued to call at Millport, using the inner berth adjacent to the goods shed, as had her predecessors. In her latter years she always had an unkempt appearance, especially when compared to *Saxon*. Her funnel in those years should have been yellow and black, but always appeared to be off-cream and black. She sailed last in the summer of 1957 and was broken up at Port Glasgow.

From that time Millport cargo was handled by one of the "general purpose" ferries (usually known as car ferries), *Arran, Cowal* and *Bute*, on a service from Wemyss Bay on Mondays, Wednesdays and Fridays. These ships encouraged car traffic too, their lifts giving much easier access for cars than by the traditional method used by *Talisman* and her paddle predecessors. This had entailed driving on to the steamers over open

Loading a car onto P. S. Mercury in the 1930s.
courtesy C.R.S.C.

planks of wood. A fairly nerve-racking business and one which was only possible at some stages of the tide. Nerve-racking for drivers, but greatly enjoyed by spectators!

In time much of the cargo traffic was containerised and was towed on and off the ferries by little tractorised vehicles.

With the opening of Cumbrae Slip in 1972 most of the cargo has been diverted to the ferries using that route. The final car ferry calls at the Old Pier were in 1977, when large caravans were landed by the *Cowal*.

The Fishing Boats

THE earliest boats on the island must have worked as fishing boats, though there is no detailed information regarding them till the early 18th century. Between 1707 and 1712 the following sailing fishing boats were based on the island:- *Comrade* (3 tons burthen); Janet I (7 tons); *Janet II* (6 tons); *Margaret* (12 tons); *Martin* (6 tons).

The New Statistical Account of 1840 mentioned that weaving was the principal employment of the town, but was silent on fishing. A reminiscence published in the *Largs & Millport Weekly News* of July 30th 1887 said: "Up to 40 years ago the sight of 20 or 30 fishing boats of the local fleet on a summer evening . . ." Most of the men "left boat for loom in the winter."

Annan's photographs of the Harbour in the 1900s show five double-ended rowing/sailing fishing boats with Greenock registration numbers. By the end of the 1914-18 war three Millport families were still fishing — McLachlans, McNeils and Wrights. All used this type of 4-oar rowing boat with lugsail. They were about 20 feet long and had a six feet beam. Peter and Dan McLachlan had *Jane Stewart*; the McNeil brothers Lachie and John had *Flora*, and Alex Wright had his boat *Margaret Wright* (built for him by Mauchline for £20). The boat names were family ones. The long-line fishing which they used must have been monotonous cold work. Using mussels for bait, they often fished for whiting at night in Fintry Bay, but also went as far afield as Inchmarnock.

Alex Wright was also known as a photographer but his fishing was done in the off-season. His son Ronnie began to help in 1923, and later when he went "deep sea", his younger brother Sandy and John helped too. Dan McLachlan's son Donnie began to help in the family boat at about the same time. Later they bought the *Gem*, a somewhat larger boat with a petrol/paraffin engine. *Gem* was used in summer for trips and in winter for fishing. She in turn was succeeded by *Maree* which they used till 1939. During World War II she was laid up in Mauchline's boatyard. By 1939 Donnie was fishing alone, while his widowed mother and later his wife Isobel, sold fish in a shop at the head of the Strathwherry Pier. The McNeils too acquired a larger motor boat in the 1920s, the *Dorothy,* which was used for visitors trips, but they gradually moved their attention from fishing to boathiring, generally based at the Leck Pier.

In the years after World War II Donnie McLachlan fished on alone, apparently the last of the Millport fishermen, but in reality most of the fish sold in the family shop was imported from the east coast fisheries. Donnie and Isobel worked together in the shop and his local catches augmented the basic trade. He had four

Rowing fishing boats moored in the harbour (1898-1905). courtesy Annan & Co.

small open fishing launches in turn. After the sale of *Maree* there was a varnished wooden launch called *Merlin* which bore prominently his registration number — GK47.

In 1957 he and Alex Hunter each purchased for £25 a ship's lifeboat from the scrapyard in Troon. They had come from a Heysham ferry probably *Duke of Argyll* or one of her sister ships. The two lifeboats were brought to the island on the deck of the puffer *Saxon* and were renovated together by the two men at Hunter's West Bay Slip Yard. McLachlan's was painted green topped with brown and named *Merlin*, replacing the older launch of the same name. Hunter's boat was painted blue and named *Southwind II*. About 1960 Donnie bought a second launch the *Speedwell*, a Canadian-built launch which had previously sailed from Largs and had been bought subsequently by Farquhar Roberts. Donnie rechristened her *Kestrel* and repainted her in the same colours as the new *Merlin*. *Kestrel* and *Merlin* were run together through the 1960s and into the 1970s, with Donnie's nephew Campbell, often working the smaller boat. Donnie's final boat was *Jane Stewart,* another double ended boat, though carvel-built this time, which he had resurrected from a hull laid up on Loch Striven-side. *Jane Stewart* was Donnie's "retirement" boat and each summer of the late 70s and early 80s he and Isobel went a lengthy West Highland Cruise.

Donnie himself was a remarkable boatman. For years the island's doctors turned to him for help in transporting dangerously ill patients to the mainland and a waiting ambulance, if there was an emergency overnight. Despite trips in very wild weather, he never let them down. As the years went by he fished less, and diversified his activities. He ran a regular early Sunday morning run with newspapers from Fairlie to Cumbrae and Rothesay. Then there were fishing party charters from the mainland and ferry trips to and from Wee Cunbrae. When Alex Hunter relinquished the lease on the West Bay Slip Yard, Donnie also took that over.

Two of the fishermen of that generation became known in the world at large. Ronnie Wright became Commodore of the Union Castle Line and Donnie McLachan was elected Provost of Millport.

During the 1950s other fishermen appeared on the island to operate the vessels of the Scottish Marine Biological Association. Alex Soutar a Johnshaven man had responded to an advertisement for crew to man the S.M.B.A. ship *Calanus*. In turn he persuaded his cousin Robert McBay to join him on the west coast. At first the *Calanus* (a converted MFV) was moored in Balloch Bay and the men had to cycle daily from their homes in Millport. Later, when the smaller *Mizpah* was purchased, she was moored in Millport Bay. The punt for *Mizpah* was specially built by James Mauchline and was regularly moored overnight in the shelter of the stone part of Millport Pier. McBay was skipper of the *Mizpah* (BA11) for many years till his retirement in the mid 1970s. Subsequent to her stranding in Millport Bay in

Millport fishing boats shelter in the harbour, Nov. 1991, L. to R. Norvic Lass, Nancy Glen, Silver Sky, Aplysia, (Aora at mooring). courtesy Walter Kerr.

1977, two new vessels were built by the University Marine Station (SMBA had moved to Dunstaffnage in 1970). Both are regularly moored in Millport Bay and their (now motorised) punt is moored in the same place as before. The new boats are called *Aplysia* and *Aora*. The latter has a Waverley style funnel! (red, white and black).

In his spare time Robert McBay was also a salmon fisher. Near Farland Point he set up large nets from his long open boat *Hilda*. McBay had leased the salmon rights for the island, and also smoked fish in one of the outbuildings behind The College where he and his family stayed for many years.

One of the younger Millport men, Alistair Roberts, was interested in fishing on the Clyde for a livelihood, and in 1975 began running the cobble *Marion* for fishing parties and later for commercial fishing. He learned much from Robert McBay, who in his retirement enjoyed showing the younger man the detailed work of making and mending nets, and other intricate parts of his craft. In 1985 Alistair bought the larger *Nancy Glen* and has continued fishing with her till the present day. Stuart McIntyre's *Norvic Lass* joined the Millport fishing fleet in 1987 and Leadbetter's *Silver Sky* in 1991. Most of the trade of these boats is in prawns. Catches are usually landed at Largs Pier but their home base is Millport Pier. So in 1992 once more there are three fishing boats sailing from the island.

Storm

courtesy Walter Kerr. *After storm, showing lifted planks.*

The Boathirers

For over 100 years the Millport boathirers were an important part of the local scene. They provided a need that now seems largely to have evaporated. Mostly their trade was conducted from one or other of the small piers or jetties in Millport Bay, but they would all at some point depend on the facilities of the Old Pier. Whether it was for shelter in bad weather, or for landing passengers from motor launches when the tide was very low, or for launching small boats, or for regular traffic, the Old Pier was a constant dependable factor in their calculations.

One important name appearing first in April, 1893, was that of Colin Mauchline, who wrote to the Council applying for a stance for letting boats on Strathwherry Pier. The Mauchline family soon moved to the island, but were never really accepted by the others. By June 1894, the disagreements with W. B. Wallace, also a boathirer, had reached the stage of letters to the Council. In 1896 C. Wallace, A. Hunter and W. McNicol were all hiring from the Leck Pier, but by 1898 the Hunters had moved to the Strathwherry and the fighting had become more intense.

(Extract of letter from Neil Hunter, 28th June, 1898)

"During the busiest part of the season, parties have frequently to wait no inconsiderable time before getting off shore, and as sitting accommodation, ample at all other times, proves then rather limited, many even elderly ladies and gentlemen are compelled to remain on their feet. For this reason a seat at the head of the Strathwherry Pier is almost a necessity. . ."

(Extract of letter from Colin Mauchline, 29th June)

". . . but (Mr Hunter) has since placed a form where the box was, thus leaving me in as bad a position as before. There seems but one alternative left me, and that is to obtain your permission to put down a similar seat alongside his, and thus put us on equal terms. . ."

Such like quarrels were to continue without let or hindrance for 60 years. This Hunter-Mauchline feud has become part of Millport legend, but disputes about who had stolen a baling can from whom could still erupt as late as the 1950s. In 1992 one can only regret the situation which arose, for while the Hunters came of a line of expert boatmen, the Mauchlines built splendid boats.

Each family had its strengths. It seems a pity that they could not co-exist more cheerfully.

By the mid-1900s, a small additional jetty had been built to the south west of the head of Strathwherry. This was principally to accommodate Mauchline's first motor launch, *Triumph,* which appeared about 1909. Then the Hunters built a parallel jetty for their motor boats, the first of which was the launch, *Valetta* (perhaps named after the Earl of Glasgow's *Valetta* of 1856). To replace the first *Triumph,* Mauchline built the larger *Triumph II,* and Hunter acquired the *Sunbeam* —a motorised conversion of a rowing life-boat from Cullercoats. The largest boat ever built on the island was Mauchline's *pièce de résistance, Triumph III,* a broad carvel-built launch with a Board of Trade Certificate for 58 passengers. Hunter's reply to this in 1934 was *Cramond Brig,* a 56 foot enclosed launch from the Firth of Forth, with a Certificate for 100 passengers. *Cramond Brig* could really be classed as a small steamer, and, when on the ferry runs to Largs along with *Triumph III,* she began to affect the passenger numbers on the railway steamers. *Wee Cumbrae* was built by the C. P. S. as a direct reply to this excellent private competition.

By the 1930s the McNeil family were moving from fishing to hiring, and they too had a launch, the *Dorothy,* sailing from the Leck. Harry Little and his father ran boats from their own wooden jetty slightly west of the Leck. Harry had *Jean* and *Grace* (and later *Grace II),* which were used both for public trips and for communication with the lighthouse on Wee Cumbrae. The largest Little boat was *Spindrift* built about 1935 by McLean of Govan. Finally, Mr. Dunan ran a fleet of small boats from his own jetty opposite the East Church. He also had a 25 foot launch, *Glenburn.* All these launches ran trips to various tourist attractions in the area: Wee Cumbrae (with time ashore at the lighthouse), Kilchattan Bay, Round the Cumbraes, Kerrycroy, Portencross. Another important and lucrative service was the special run done in conjuction with the evening shows at Barrfields Pavilion, Largs.

Of course, the launches were the icing on the cake. The bread and butter trade was the hiring of individual rowing boats from the piers and jetties. Then, just before the outbreak of World War II, Mauchline introduced a novelty which was to prove very popular—the "Drive-Yourself" motor boat. His first two, *Gay* and *Joy* —appeared in the summer of 1939.

Sadly, the fleet of launches which resumed service on the island in 1946 was greatly depleted. *Cramond Brig* did not re-appear, nor did Mauchline's *Triumph II.* In addition, Harry Little quite soon withdrew from boathiring altogether to concentrate on his other business, as a cobbler. His last boat, *Spindrift,* was sold to Saltcoats, and was to be seen in Douglas, Isle of Man,

Triumph 1 at extra jetty at Strathwherry pre 1914. Notice planking on main jetty. *courtesy J. McFarlane.*

Cramond Brig and Triumph II at extra jetties at Strathwherry, 1930s.
courtesy Ian Brown.

in the early 1980s. The early motor launch jetties at the Strathwherry Pier were not renovated, and Little's jetty disappeared. However, a slimmed down fleet of boats continued to give great pleasure to many during the 1950s. Many more "Drive-Yourselves" were built. Alex Hunter (better known as 'Scud') built *Fay, Frolic* and *Fidget* while Jimmy Mauchline built *Randy* and *Dandy,* and finally *Ranter* and *Rambler*. Jimmy Calder, who had taken over Dunan's jetty, introduced *Dot* and *Dash,* and, in addition to these "Drive-Yourselves", brought out a real novelty, *Flash,* a wooden-hulled speed-boat. McNeil's fleet declined until they stopped altogether in 1955. In their place Charles Wilson, a taxi-hirer, began also to hire small boats at the Leck Pier. While Mauchline continued with the big *Triumph III,* Alex Hunter also had a small cream and brown launch, *Southwind* which has a Certificate for 12. *Sunbeam,* Hunter's remaining pre-war boat, could carry 35.

As described in the chapter on the fishing boats, McLachlan and Hunter each purchased a lifeboat from a cross-channel steamer in 1957. Hunter's boat was painted in the same blue as *Sunbeam,* and was christened *Southwind II.* The *Southwind* was sold to Bobby Wilkie, a private owner who re-named her *Westwind.* The new boat, like her predecessor, had a Certificate for 12, and was used to supplement the cruises or fishing parties taken by *Sunbeam*. She was usually helmed by Jimmy Clydesdale, a pawky Glasgow man who became Scud's assistant when he and his wife moved to the island.

Writing of Jimmy Clydesdale brings to mind the scene at the Strathwherry in the late 1950s. At the head of the jetty were two huts, one for each owner, which were swapped over annually lest either should gain an advantage over the other. A "form" was placed outside each hut, on which were seated men and boys shelling cockles for fishing parties. Down the pier small boats of each fleet were moored, bow-in, in readiness for custom. Earlier in the morning, young boys would have helped by bailing out a boat each, in return for the fun of sailing it into the Strathwherry. All the boats bar one were varnished clinker ones. The exception was Mauchline's punt, a large rowing boat painted blue, and generally reckoned to be the oldest boat of either fleet. It was said that she had been repaired so many times that only a small length of the keel of the original boat was left. On a calm evening there were competitions among the Mauchline boys to find how many people she could carry without sinking. The record was said to be in the upper twenties! The *Sunbeam* and *Triumph* were brought into Strathwherry in the early afternoon in time for the afternoon cruise at 2.40 p.m., alternately to Kilchattan or the Lighthouse. While the owners were away on these cruises, their assistants, Jimmy Clydesdale and one of Jimmy Mauchline's sisters (Maud or Tina), held sway over the fleet of small boats and small boys, and the disputes and arguments continued unabated.

Owing to poor health, Mauchline retired from hiring in 1959. The front of the family house in Guildford Street was converted into a sweet shop, and the fleet of boats and the Kames Street boatyard were sold. *Triumph III* went to Largs to be re-named *Golden Triumph* by Harry Hart.

The three remaining boathirers compensated for Mauchline's demise by expanding their fleet of small boats. Alex Hunter, in particular, built a few more fine "Drive-Yourself" motor boats: *Sheena, Sandra* and finally *Sonia*. However, he too was ageing and *Southwind II* was sold, again to Wilkie, without replacement in 1967. *Sunbeam* was sold to Gourock owners the following year. The small boats were bought by a former employee, Stuart McIntyre, while Hunter's lease on the West Bay boatyard was passed to Donnie McLachlan. At about the same time Jimmy Calder's business was bought by a Glasgow man, Robert Liddell, who ran it for only one season, 1967, before abandoning it in favour of running Whinfield Dairy.

Thus in the 1970s, only Wilson at the Leck and McIntyre at the Strathwherry remained. Clearly the economic viability of boat-hiring was in question. Even the existing owners were not solely boat-hirers. Each had other work in the winter.

The one encouraging feature was the continuing popularity of the fishing party. McLachlan had parties booked every weekend of the year, mostly taken from Fairlie Pier. In an attempt to develop this trade, Sandy Wright Jr., son of Ronnie Wright, bought a Weymouth launch *Endeavour* in 1972. Wright advertised public fishing parties from the Old Pier, and also undertook charter work. He added the year-round Sunday paper run to Millport and Rothesay which McLachlan had carried out until the autumn of 1973. To provide a back-up launch he also bought *Endurance* in 1974.

McIntyre also took an interest in this fishing-party

trade, especially after he bought McLachlan's *Kestrel* and *Merlin,* in 1974. At the same time he took on the lease of the West Bay Slip Yard and began to upgrade the facilities there quite markedly. While McLachlan had been content to make the yard cover its costs, the younger man wanted to obtain a significant part of his income from the slipping and storing of private boats. So new rails were laid, a new winch installed, and large areas of the yard were given a proper concrete finish for the first time. Soon the yard was full of laid-up boats in the winter, and McIntyre was also involved in the lifting and laying of moorings in the Bay. Following a particularly bad season in 1978, McIntyre and Wilson began to withdraw from the traditional clinker boats at the two hiring piers.

In 1979 Stuart McIntyre, in partnership with his brother Peter, took over the hiring business of Harry Hart in Largs. As well as the fleet of small boats, they also acquired two launches *Golden Spur* and *Golden Triumph* (formerly Mauchline's *Triumph III).* The two brothers ran the double business for five years and at one time had five motor launches — *Golden Triumph, Golden Spur, Stardrift, Starcrest,* and *Kestrel*. Unfortunately, despite all their efforts, the hiring trade became still more diffcult in the 1980s. The changing regulations of the Board of Trade made expenses ever greater, and the public seemed reluctant to pay increased charges. More devastating still was the decline in fishing party trade. The McIntyres withdrew from Largs in 1984, and most of their launches were laid up or sold. Peter became boatman for Mr. Kaye of Wee Cumbrae and Stuart tried another tack by buying the fishing boat, *Norvic Lass,* in 1987. He also tried the newer style of fibre glass boats, the Wave Bobs, in 1985, and the Pedalos in 1986. Finally he bought a number of new fibre glass rowing boats which had been tried by Tam Gledhill for a season or two.

In October, 1985, Sandy Wright withdrew from the Sunday paper run and sold his remaining boat to Donald Patrick, who carried on the run. However *Endeavour* was badly damaged in the summer of 1986 and was laid up in Millport Harbour. In the same year Sandy Wright formed Cumbrae Coaches to operate on the Cumbrae Slip to Millport route, in oppositon to Millport Motors.

Golden Triumph was sold in 1988 to owners in Donaghadee. Her stay in Ireland was short, however, and was followed by a spell at Tobermory. She is now based at Anstruther. *Kestrel* was wrecked in September 1988 while helping the small steamer *Saint Gerrans* which had run aground on the rocks outside the Outer Eilean.

And so the hiring trade in Millport today is all but dead. Apart from a few weeks in mid-summer when Wave Bobs and Pedalos are hired from the middle of Newton Bay beach, nothing remains. Stuart McIntyre, the last of the hirers, now earns his living mostly from other work.

Pier Worthies

OF COURSE in the busy times in the past the Pier had staff of its own to organise passengers, goods and steamers. The last Piermaster of the Millport Pier and Harbour Company was Alex Caldwell (Acky Peevy), and he continued with the Town Council after 1905. He was a kenspeckle figure in the community and very thorough in his duties. In the 1920s his staff consisted of Jenny Kerr and Lizzie McWha, both well known turnstile attendants. Alex Caldwell must have had a demanding job. On the busiest days he would have to organise five or six groups of trippers, each several hundred strong and ensure that each group boarded the correct steamer. There might be three steamers loading passengers at one time. Nevertheless, Caldwell remained Piermaster until about the middle of World War II.

At this time all goods were barrowed on and off steamers and the carting agents, Messrs Stewart, had quite a number of staff. In the office were Misses Lizzie and Jean Stewart, with help in summer from an L.M.S.

Horse carriages on Pier, 1920s? Third from right A. Caldwell, Piermaster. courtesy Museum of the Cumbraes

clerk. The carting side was run by James Stewart with the assistance of Neil McPail, Willie Johnston, Andy Johnston (no relation) and Jimmy McLachlan. The men operated horse drawn carts and lorries to deliver goods on the day of their arrival at the pier. At the busiest times, the change of fortnight, the local contractor McIntyre Brothers helped as well.

Caldwell's successor as Piermaster was Freddie Morgan, who was also in charge of the Cartage now taken over by the Council. Morgan was a very dapper little man who is remembered particularly for being fair with his workforce and liaising well between the Council and his staff. In Morgan's time the office staff were Mary Barr and Betty Bone. Gerry Smart was foreman, Bud Finlayson was checker, and other members of staff were Dan McGregor, Joe Morgan, John Meechan, Stuart Marshall and Jimmy Stevenson.

Freddie Morgan died in office and was replaced by William McKay, who in turn was succeeded by Robert Miller. Miller was the last Millport Piermaster and he went about 1972, when most of the traffic was directed to the Cumbrae Slip Ferry.

When we look back at the 1920s, the scene at the Pier was a bustling one. When passengers disembarked, carriages, taxis and later buses waited to take them to their lodgings. Jack Shearer operated a fleet of horse-drawn cabs, and also a fourteen-seater horse bus for runs round the island. He continued with his horse carriage well into 1950s. Motor taxis were run by a few operators: Jimmy Risk, Bobby Frame, Willie Burnie, Bob Black and Johnny Morrison. Willie Burnie also operated the island's first motor bus.

Pier lorry loaded with hampers, and "the squad", 1950s.

On his retiral Willie Burnie sold out to the Morrison Brothers. In the 1950s the Morrisons ran two Bedford buses and a Commer. The Morrison firm, called Millport Motors, also ran mini-buses from the Pier to Kirkton Caravan Site and now are one of the two operators on the run to Cumbrae Slip. The other firm, Cumbrae Coaches, is run by Ronnie Wright's son, Sandy.

In post-war years Charlie Wilson and his family were well-known taxi operators.

Other Cumbrae Piers

Balloch Pier

AWARE of the difficulties caused by the exposure to rough weather of Millport Pier, the first Provost of Millport, local benefactor, the Earl of Glasgow, had a new Pier built on the east shore of the island in 1872. There, winds which made Millport Bay difficult would have little effect. He returned to the traditional ferry point at Douncraig in Balloch Bay and had an iron pier built on the promontory there.

The *North British Daily Mail* of 5th June, 1872 reported the opening thus: "By the kindness of Captain James Gillies, of the Wemyss Bay Steamboat Company, the I.O.G.T. Lodges of Largs and Millport were treated to an excursion on Monday evening. The steamer *Lancelot* having the Largs Templars and friends on board, were joined at Millport by the Cumbrae Light Lodge and thereafter proceeded as far as the Garroch Head, skirted the shores of Bute as far as opposite Mount Stuart House, crossed the Firth, making the circuit of Tomont End, and landed at the new Pier at the ferry, when the procession formed and marched, preceded by the Largs and Millport brass bands, as far as the cottages newly built for the officials, thence returned to the quay, forming a cordon round the ancient mound near its head. Bro D. McLaren, W.C.T.C.L.L., was called upon to preside. In a short but pithy address he referred to the great kindness of the Earl of Glasgow in allowing the Templars to land first upon the Pier, and also to his Lordship's liberality not only towards Cumbrae, in forming new roads along its shores and braes, and in building a new Pier for the accommodation of the farmers etc., but also towards all his other estates since his Lordship came into possession. He then called for three hearty cheers for Lord Glasgow, which were given vociferously. Three cheers having been given for Captain James Gillies, Messrs James Brow, C.E., Wishart & Paterson, the builders of the stone work the Chairman declared the Pier opened, under the name of Balloch Bay Pier. The company then re-embarked and having called at Largs to land their friends there, arrived at Millport about 9 o'clock, all highly delighted with their trip. It is understood that the Pier is still strictly private and any parties wishing to land must first apply to W. J. Armstrong, Esq., Fairlie, his Lordship' factor."

The Earl's intention was to help the islanders, so doubtless the private nature of the Pier soon disappeared, and it was used as an emergency pier and as a destination for occasional evening cruises. There is one mention in the *Largs and Millport Weekly News*, showing a "Saturdays only" call, in November 1878, by the Wemyss Bay steamers.

The Pier's lack of popularity seems at this date quite odd. Had Balloch Pier survived into the late 20th century, it might have become the main landing point on the island instead of the Tattie Pier. However, the steep hills of the Ferry Road between Balloch Pier and the town were not popular in days of horse transport, and the Pier was not greatly used. By the late 1880s the Pier was said to be in poor condition, probably through lack of maintenance following the Earl's bankruptcy in 1885. When Keppel Pier was built in 1888, it superseded Balloch as the emergency pier for the island and Balloch became redundant. The last record of its use is in February, 1892, when an extremely high tide forced the winter steamer to call there instead of at either of the other steamer piers.

The ironwork was removed about 1900, leaving only the walled approach.

Keppel Pier

AS the town of Millport expanded eastward and westward along Millport Bay during the 1860s and 1870s, the distance between the newest villas and the Old Pier gradually increased. This was particularly true of the properties on the east side of Kames Bay on Marine Parade. Some houses were over a mile from the Pierhead, so, to improve the accessibility of this part of the town, there was a suggestion that a new pier be built just beyond Keppel Point.

About 1875 discussions took place about the project with the landowner, the Earl of Glasgow and he agreed to make the necessary land available, but although there was much local support, the plan did not proceed at that time.

After the financial collapse of the Glasgow family and the consequent repair problems at Balloch Pier, the Keppel project was revived. The scheme had always envisaged that a pier at Keppel Point would be accessible in almost all weathers and would thus be an alternative to the Old Pier in stormy weather, as well as providing easy access to the east end of the town. This would also be an improvement on Balloch Pier in stormy weather. There were two public meetings in quick succession on 19th December 1887 and 14th January 1888 to discuss the matter. At the latter a committee was established and shares in the Keppel Pier Company were soon being sold. The Marquis of Bute, successor to Lord Glasgow as landowner, leased the necessary ground free of rent. On April 4th 1888, construction estimates of Messrs Kennedy of Partick were accepted and building went ahead rapidly.

There were problems, of course. Difficulties with rocky outcrop caused the line of the pier to be moved eastward by 20 feet, which in turn caused the approach gangway to be lengthened by the same distance. Then in

Marchioness of Graham arriving at Keppel Pier, winter in the 1950s. N. B. Millport Motors' Commer bus and Cartage Dept. Karrier lorry. courtesy Walter Kerr.

July there was an accident with one of the cranes which delayed work for five days. The New Pier was opened on 18th August by the paddler *Adela* of Captain Campbell's Wemyss Bay Company and the shareholders were taken for a cruise round Wee Cumbrae.

The design of Keppel Pier was typical of many small Clyde piers of this time, being built in a T shape with berthing for one steamer. Other piers of this style included Kilchattan Bay, Arrochar, Tighnabruaich and Kilcreggan. Only the last two are still in use. Latterly Keppel Pier had a few variations to the usual structure: the main face was not a straight line, but rather in two halves, the south one at right angles to the gangway, the other at a more acute angle, which helped steamers to avoid Keppel Point to the south of the Pier.

Keppel was always quite different from Millport Pier. The fishermen and the boat-hirers made little use of it. It was rarely used for mooring steamers overnight. Somehow there was little inclination to linger at Keppel, while the older Pier always had its share of spectators. Yet it was an asset to the island, and was bought by the Town Council in 1905 as part of the deal for Millport Pier. It was an excellent alternative for passengers in southerly gales and in the days of the larger steamers it was frequently in use in rough weather in winter. Many a day the "Boat at Keppel" placard was seen at the Old Pier and weary travellers boarded the bus for the 1½ mile trip. The steamer timetables warned that "in the event of tide or weather conditions being unfavourable for calling at Millport (Old Pier) a call will be made at Keppel 7 minutes later". There was always ample depth of water at Keppel, even at low tide, so, from the late 1920s, when the large turbine steamers began to be scheduled to call at the island on their long distance cruises, the difficulties of navigating such deep-draughted ships in Millport Bay were abandoned in favour of an easy call at Keppel.

When the Robertson Marine Station was founded in 1896, most of its visitors would land at Keppel, and when Sir John Clark presented the yacht *Mermaid* to the Station, it also used the pier. In turn, the Marine Station boats, *Nautilus, Calanus* and *Mizpah,* used Keppel Pier for landing specimens. The Station also used the Pier for other purposes: a tide gauge was fixed behind the south end of the Pier close to the wooden steps in 1931. After World War II the platform for underwater research was usually anchored behind the north end of the Pier. On walking down the Pier in the '50s and '60s one often found ropes attached to it. At the other ends were nets trailing through the current, accumulating microscopic marine life. The structure of the Pier itself became famous for the profusion of sea anemones which grew on its lateral beams. A new tide gauge in a substantial concrete shelter was built to the south of the gangway in the 1960s.

During World War II an anti-submarine net was

laid across Fairlie Roads just south of Keppel Pier. This net precluded steamers sailing round Farland Point into Millport Bay, so, for convenience, during wartime winters, the Arran steamer based at Fairlie maintained the Cumbrae connection too, using Keppel Pier. As the ship involved was often one of the large turbines, either Glen *Sannox* or *Duchess of Argyll,* the use of Keppel suited their deep draught.

By 1948 Keppel was in need of considerable repair and it was out of use for some months during 1949 undergoing major overhaul.

After the 1951 season the long decline of Keppel began. As part of the rationalisation of the steamer services that was happening at the time, the Millport steamer ceased regular calls at Keppel, so its only scheduled use was by summer excursion steamers. Its function as an alternative bad weather pier continued, however. The number of calls until the end of October of that year was 2069, while a year later it was a mere 812.

When the new car ferry, *Glen Sannox,* was being built in 1957, the C.S.P. approached Millport Town Council about the possibility of upgrading Keppel Pier to take the new Arran Ferry on a regular basis on her way to and from Fairlie. The Council rejected the idea, and as the new ferry was too large to use the Old Pier on a regular basis, the steamer company had to abandon the attempt to use the same ship for sailing to Cumbrae and Arran.

In the '60s, when car traffic to Cumbrae was growing, a car ferry unloading at the Old Pier could seriously delay the schedule of the regular passenger steamers, so Keppel Pier was frequently used as an alternative.

When the Cumbrae Slip service was begun in 1972 Keppel had already been demoted to an "emergency only" pier. Repairs were needed and could not be justified. In 1972, therefore, excursion steamers simply by-passed Keppel, and in August of that year it was offered to the Marine Station for £1500. The final steamer call was made on 5th May 1973 by *Queen Mary II* while on her 40 year Anniversary Cruise on charter to Clyde River Steamer Club. Shortly after, the pier passed to the Marine Station whom it served for about 12 years more. Little substantial maintenance was done, but wear and tear from the Station's own boats was very much less than from the heavier steamers. Perhaps Keppel's final moment of glory was the occasion of the visit by H.M. the Queen Mother, on June 5th, 1979. The Royal Yacht, *Britannia,* anchored off the Pier and a Royal Barge landed Her Majesty at the steps behind the south end. After a visit to the University Marine Station, she left by the same means, and the *Britannia* sailed to the Hunterston Ore Terminal.

Eventually the condition of the Pier did give cause for concern, and rather than renovate the old Pier, it was decided to build a new pier slightly to the north. The new steel structure was built by George Leslie and Company of Barrhead, and when the gangway from the shore had progressed far enough, the north end of the old Keppel Pier was removed. On completion of the new Keppel Pier the *Aplysia* and *Aora* deserted their old home, and Leslie and Company was left to demolish the 1888 structure.

The Leck Pier

THE Leck Pier, beside the Crocodile Rock, was built around a natural rock formation, and was less used than the Strathwherry. The Council Minutes of 19/4/1893 note a decision that at its lower end the Leck should be levelled and widened. In 1896 it was used by boat-hirers C. Wallace, A. Hunter and W. McNicol, and in this century by the McNeils. Harry Little built his own jetty a little to the west. Later Wilson took over, but all hiring here has now ceased, and it is used principally as a landing point for visiting boats.

Tattie Pier — Cumbrae Slip

THIS pier was built as a goods wharf for the farms in the north of the island, particularly Portrye. It was used by puffers, the last call being made by *Spartan* in 1969 to land material for the construction of the coup at White Bay. On his early Sunday morning newspaper run in the 1960s and '70s, Donnie McLachlan used to land the papers at Tattie Pier if the tide was suitable. In the autum of 1971 Caledonian MacBrayne leased the land

Strathwherry Pier about 1870 showing both jetties and "Steamboat Row". courtesy J. McFarlane

near this Pier and constructed a concrete slip as their ferry terminal for their new service to the island, on top of the old Tattie Pier. A pity that the old name has disappeared!

The Strathwherry Pier

THIS stone jetty or pier in the Bay directly opposite Reid Street is said to have been used for gaining access to the original Revenue cutter *Cumbrae Wherry*. In the first half of the 19th century there were two jetties parallel to each other. Presumably the westerly one acted as a breakwater for the other one. In the earliest day of steamboats, when there was not a tidal pier, the steamer anchored in the shelter of the Eilans, and landed passengers on to one or other of the jetties. At that time the houses on Guildford Street opposite the head of this Pier were identical two-storey buildings, and were known locally as "Steamboat Row". The second jetty was demolished about 1871 and its stone used for infill at School Bay.

Boathiring became the principal use of the Pier during the late 19th century. At that time the top section was not solid, but planks were slung from raised piers. Some photographs show the Pier in winter with the decking removed. The Strathwherry Pier was the scene of the well-known feud between the boat-hiring families of Hunter and Mauchline. Succeeding them as boat-hirers was Stuart McIntyre in 1969, and the Pier is still used occasionally as a hiring place, though the rocky bottom does not encourage visiting boats to berth.

Spartan unloading at Tattie Pier, Aug. 1969.
courtesy Walter Kerr

Figgatoch Pier

THIS is the least-known of the island's piers. It is situated in a little bay north of Fintry Bay comparatively close to Figgatoch Farm. It comprises a few stone blocks on a convenient rocky promontory. Whether it was used perhaps for the export of quarried stone or as a farm pier is now not certain.

Coruisk at Cumbrae Slip on trial run, March 1972. Notice old Tattie Pier. Personnel left to right — Donnie McLachlan, ?, Calum Morrison, Graeme Wallace, Marie Roberts, ?, Campbell McLachlan, Alistair McMillan. courtesy Walter Kerr

Acknowledgements

THROUGHOUT the writing of this little book I have had help and encouragement wherever I have turned. When I have sought a difficult piece of information I have not been fobbed off. If my immediate victims did not know the answer, they would direct to some other poor creature who might. Yet despite my questionings I have not caught anyone running away from me. Perhaps I'm not as nimble as once I was, or perhaps I'm just lucky enough to have a few friends left!

My first thanks must go to the book's dedicatee, the late John Robertson, a remarkable Glasgow man who knew more about the industrial archaeology of West Scotland than anyone else I've ever met. Fortunately he had a gift for inspiring others, and my abiding interest in such matters was carefully fostered by him in my teens. Few books written about railways, ships and industry in Glasgow and the West of Scotland during the last forty years, fail to acknowledge John's valued assistance.

Like John, I owe a debt to the Librarians and Curators who so willingly gave of their time. Kathryn Valentine of the Museum of the Cumbraes, Judith Davenport of Cunninghame District Council's Library Headquarters and Judith Rankin of the McLean Museum, Greenock, were unfailingly obliging and helpful.

The owners of the photographs used in this book have been acknowledged in situ, but I cannot omit a special word for Walter Kerr whose collection of Cumbrae photographs must be unequalled. He has produced new copies of many photos for me and I would like to thank him most warmly for his kindness. Other photographers who have been specially kind were the three Ians: Brown, Duncan and McCrorie — a veritable Holy Trinity of Cumbrae enthusiasts!

Other friends who have advised me have included: Mr David Bowman, Mr Alex Burnie, Mr George and Mrs Grace Beagrie, Mr Duncan Campbell, Mrs Margaret Hastie, Mr David Hepburn, Mr G. E. Langmuir, Mr Ion McBay, Mr James MacFarlane, Mr Daniel McGregor, Mr David McKenzie, Mr Stuart McIntyre, Mrs Isobel McLachlan, Mr Campbell McLachlan, Mr Hugh McLachlan, Captain Sween McSween, Mr Sandy Morton, Mrs Jenny Orr, Mr Alistair Roberts, Mr Donald Swan, Mr Bobby Wilkie, Captain R. M. Wright and Mr Alexander G. Wright.

Mr Eric Graham has been a most helpful correspondent, giving me details of 18th century shipping. Miss Sarah Goldie has given discreet but invaluable help in matters of syntax and construction.

But finally I have to take sole responsibility for having written the book. If there are faults, they are mine. If the errors make you angry, consider the reasons for your not having written the book yourself. If my mistakes make you laugh, please let me know, so that I can share the joke and put your corrections into my copy too.

Bibliography

New Statistical Account of Scotland: Bute	1840
History of the County of Bute — Eaton Reid	1864
Guide Book to the Cumbraes — W. Lytteil	1886
The Clyde Passenger Steamer — Williamson	1904
The Victorian Summer of the Clyde Steamers — Paterson	1969
The Golden Years of the Clyde Steamers — Paterson	1972
The Millport Route — McCrorie	1974
Scottish Sail — Simper	1975
Millport and the Cumbraes — Campbell	1975
Minutes of Millport Town Council	1864-1975
Minutes of the Keppel Pier Company	1887-1905
The Largs Advertiser	1870s
Largs and Millport Weekly News	1977-present